Exhausted

Thirty days to rethink and rediscover rest

Nathan Oates & David Timms

Exhausted: Thirty days to rethink and rediscover rest
Copyright © 2024 by Nathan Oates & David Timms.
All rights reserved.

All Scripture quotations are from the HOLY BIBLE, NEW INTERNATIONAL VERSION® Copyright © 1973, 1978, 1984, 2011 by International Bible Society. Used by permission of Zondervan Publishing House. All rights reserved.

All emphasis in Scripture is by the authors.

No part of this book may be reproduced or transmitted in any form or by any means, electronic or mechanical, including photocopying, or any information storage or retrieval system, without prior permission in writing from the author. The only exception is brief quotations in printed reviews.

Emmaus Artifacts
Lincoln, CA

Library of Congress Cataloging-in-Publication Data
Nathan Oates & David Timms
Exhausted: Thirty days to rethink and rediscover rest

ISBN-13: 979-8-321-69585-2

Printed in the United States of America

Cover Design: Sienna Oates

Table of Contents

Introduction		5
1.	How did we get here?	8
2.	What is rest?	12
3.	The gift of rest	15
4.	When do we need rest?	18
5.	Bone-tired and stressed-out	21
6.	A design plan or design flaw?	24
7.	False assumptions about rest	27
8.	Perceived hindrances to rest	30
9.	I'm not ready to rest	33
10.	I'm not able to rest	37
11.	I'm not willing to rest	41
12.	Human machines vs. human beings	44
13.	Ending slavery	48
14.	Be still in the storm	51
15.	Rest for the soul	56
16.	The rest stop is not our destination	60
17.	Rest from the noise	63
18.	Herman Melville's harpooner	66
19.	Days that start at night	69
20.	Forced rest	73
21.	A yoke of rest	76
22.	A yoke of companionship	80
23.	A yoke of grace	83
24.	Rest and our identity	86
25.	Rest and personality	89
26.	Harmful proverbs	92
27.	Helpful metaphors	96
28.	Simple practices; difficult habits	100
29.	Eternal rest	105
30.	Back to Jesus	108

Introduction

We are probably not the people who should write this book. We've not perfected the art of resting. We struggle with rest and restoration as much as anyone else. We understand the drive for productivity, the allure of distraction, and the reality of stress. Perhaps that's precisely why we're writing it.

Here's why we feel so compelled. We are increasingly sure that we need change, and that we are not alone in this. Most of us are weary and worn out far too much of the time. As a culture, we live on an emotional edge too often. We are sleep deprived, frequently stressed, and constantly tired. More than that, we're exhausted. Our bodies don't like it. Our relationships suffer because of it. And our souls are more deeply depleted than we know.

If none of this rings true for you, then go no further. Please pass this book on to a friend or family member. There are plenty of people in your orbit who need a fresh understanding of rest and a way to rethink and rediscover it.

This journey for us began most seriously in Fall 2023 with a four-week sermon series at Emmaus Church Community around the theme of *Rest*. As we engaged with members of the church community week after week, we consistently heard: "Wow! This is really needed, challenging, and helpful." We also discovered that weekly small group conversations between Sundays had too little time to fully unpack the nuances and needs that people identified. It was a hot button for so many of us.

This whole experience begged a question: Would it be possible and helpful to dive deeper and create a short guide for ourselves and others to rethink and rediscover rest?

What follows is our deeper journey and we invite you to join us.

How to use this book

You might use this book in various ways.

1. You might see this as a 30-day journey to better self-awareness and personal change. Take just three to five minutes each day to read a chapter, ponder it, and perhaps journal about it.

2. Or, make this a different kind of journey. Skip around between the chapters, as you

like. If a heading sparks your curiosity, head there right away. You will not need spoiler alerts. The book does not rise to a great crescendo with final fireworks. Wouldn't that be ironic?

3. Or read this with some trusted friends. Meet with them for a season and chat about what you found helpful, controversial, or impossible. Verbal processing can be enormously helpful. It helps clarify ideas and makes them stick. Conversations also have a way of gently providing clarity and building some accountability. What we share with each other we tend to expect of each other.

4. Or, finally, you might be looking for material to teach someone else or fit into a paper, article, sermon, study, or other context. That's great. The process of researching, writing, and teaching often has a way of sneaking up on us and touching our own souls unawares.

However you choose to use this book, we hope that these short chapters will encourage and stimulate you to rethink rest and experience some fresh degree of restoration.

Day 1
How did we get here?

Do you feel wrung out, fatigued, or weary *some* of the time? Perhaps you experience exhaustion *all* the time, and you've grown accustomed to it and resigned yourself to it.

Too much to do? Too busy? Too many demands? Too little rest? Sleepless? Stressed? Run down? On the edge?

Whether you are studying at school, parenting young children, building a career, handling chronic illness, preparing for retirement, caring for someone who is frail, or juggling a host of other demands, life's pressure can feel relentless. We belong to a bone-weary, stressed-out society. No wonder we turn so rapidly to distractions or drugs for relief; little wonder that we hole up in our apartments or homes to escape with movies, gaming, or web-surfing. Our batteries feel depleted. We're running on fumes so much of the time.

Have you fantasized about running away to a tropical island or moving someplace where the costs are cheaper and the pace is slower? Have you been tempted to hand in your notice and go live off the grid? Who hasn't?

What we really need are legitimate options, here and now.

Collectively we probably sleep less than most generations before us. We have poorer health overall, and we're taking more medication. Help! We need rest.

In *The State of Sleep Health in America 2023* the Sleep Apnea Association reported that 50-70 million Americans have sleep disorders, and sleep deprivation is not just a private struggle but a public health concern. Indeed, poor sleepers reported 2.29 unplanned missed work days per month, versus the national average of 0.91 days. That's substantial, and it results in an estimated $44.6 billion in lost productivity each year. That's staggering.

Of course, the issue here is not to rectify the national economy but to renew our individual lives.

How did we get here?

We may have arrived at exhaustion from various directions. In the same way that multiple streams flow into a river and the water can no longer be differentiated by its source, so exhaustion may reflect many factors for each of us.

There is, of course, the simple physiological reality. Sickness, illness, or medical treatments might leave the body rather beaten down.

Others of us are exhausted because "life happens." Ask a young couple with a new baby in the house about how they are sleeping. Or someone with a new puppy! There is little choice about broken nights and muddled minds in the morning.

It's also possible that some of us have been raised with a work ethic that views rest as an occasional necessary evil. If we're resting, we are wasting time and missing opportunities.

Whatever the route, if we have arrived at deep fatigue or a weariness of the soul, it might help to frame this as a spiritual conversation. We don't need to pile guilt and shame on top of our weariness. That might tip us over the edge. But what if we saw our bodies, minds, and hearts from a stewardship perspective?

Our mental, emotional, physical, *and spiritual* health are all significantly impacted when we run ourselves into the ground. Can you identify where your own exhaustion comes from? And some ways in which your exhaustion might be undermining your flourishing life? On this first day of the journey towards rethinking and rediscovering rest, pause a moment and ask, "How did I get here?" Begin this journey with a realistic assessment of your life and lifestyle. Jot down some factors that contribute to your own exhaustion. Others may emerge later, but what stands out as obvious right now? You might even discover that one or two small changes could make an exponentially large difference over the course of the next 30 days.

Day 2
What is rest?

Rest is a good gift…from a loving God…who made us…to need rest.

If we're going to think theologically about rest…if we're going to consider the topic of rest in light of the Christian scriptures and within the context of the long history of Jewish and then Christian traditions…or, to put it very simply, if we're going to think about God and rest, we need to acknowledge that the conversation about rest is one part of a much larger conversation about *sabbath*. Sabbath is the (Hebrew) biblical word for stopping, ceasing, desisting, and resting.

The Bible's creation story is framed within the concept of time: there are six days or times of creation and on the seventh day God rested.

> By the seventh day God had finished the work he had been doing; so on the seventh day he rested (*sabbathed, ceased*) from all his work. Then God blessed the seventh day and made it holy (set it apart), because on it he rested (*sabbathed*) from all the work of creating that he had

done (Genesis 2:2-3).

Then fast forward thousands of years to the story of God giving Moses ten commands for the people of Israel who were newly freed from four hundred years of slavery. One of those commandments was: "Remember the Sabbath day by keeping it holy" (Exodus 20:8).

"Remembering the sabbath" involves much more than just rest, but rest is certainly a part of it. Sabbath is like a big, multifaceted diamond. And while we're just talking here about one facet, or one part of Sabbath, which is *rest*, it's important not to separate rest from the larger picture of Sabbath. Because if we totally separate rest from Sabbath then we end up defining rest as something very different than the thing Jesus is talking about when he says, "Come to me, all you who are weary and burdened, and I will *give you rest*."[1]

Jesus offers us rest…as we come to him.

Who's invited? Jesus says, "*All* who are weary and burdened." Yet, this invitation proves surprisingly challenging because it requires those who accept it to be real. If we're weary,

---

[1] Jesus in Matthew 11:28.

we must be honest about it. If we're burdened, we need to acknowledge it and admit it.

In other words, we could miss Jesus' invitation if we're not honest with ourselves. We could overlook this invitation if there's distance between us and Jesus.

What is rest? It is a need that God wired into us from the day of creation. It is also an invitation and a promise that is given to us by Jesus.

May we resist pseudo-solutions, temporary fixes, mindless scrolling, and quick dopamine hits…all of these counterfeit versions of rest.

How might we think and live differently if we saw rest as purposefully built into us not to limit our productivity or joy but specifically to enhance it? What might it look like to respond today to the invitation and promise of Jesus to come to him to find rest?

The biblical practice of sabbath means stopping. Meanwhile, the invitation of Jesus means intentionally turning our focus towards him. Which of these two foundational elements might need your attention today?

Day 3
The gift of rest

An orange Schwinn Sting-ray with a banana seat and monkey handle bars. The Millennium Falcon. A basketball hoop and backboard to mount on the front of the garage. These were some of the most memorable Christmas gifts I received as a kid.

Can you remember one of yours? What was your favorite childhood Christmas or birthday gift?

Here's the more important question: What did you *do* with that gift?

You could hardly wait to try it out. Right? You probably studied the details, learned how the whole thing worked; made it your own. That's what we do with much-longed-for gifts. If they're toys, we play with them. If they're tools or appliances, we use them every chance we get.

The Bible teaches us that rest is a good gift from a loving God, but we don't seem to actually believe that. If we believed rest was a gift, as tangible as those memorable Christmas gifts, we'd grab it with both hands, we'd protect it as valuable, and we'd actively engage it. We'd move past an emaciated, stripped-down view of rest as "doing nothing." Instead, resting would be something we anticipated, intentionally prepared for, and purposely embraced. We'd enjoy the gift with gratitude, not duty; with joy, not guilt. We'd unpack and discover the gift of rest.

If we didn't initially recognize or appreciate the value of rest, we'd take time to learn about it. We'd be like kids pedaling our brand new orange Schwinns with banana seats and monkey handle bars down the gravel road in our Christmas morning pajamas, stomping confidently on the coaster brakes and skidding out by the mailboxes. If we believed rest was a gift from God, we'd delight in it.

It seems we're quick to admit that we're physically weary. We're even willing to admit to those we trust that we're burdened with sadness and worry and feelings of failure. In other words, if Jesus were to ask, "Who is weary and burdened?" many of us would readily raise our hands. And yet, somehow, we are reluctant to embrace his solution; the gift of rest.

It's critical that we see, at the core, that rest is a gift. Why? Because otherwise we might approach it as a reward or a rule or an obligation or an achievement.

If we see rest as reward, we may feel that we have to earn rest; deserve it. If we see rest as a rule or an obligation, then it becomes a duty to fulfill. We have to check the box. If we see rest as an achievement or an accomplishment, then rest is something we do that makes us better or important or successful.

It's only as we understand rest biblically, as a gift, that we are freed to have a good and life-giving relationship with rest.

How have you viewed rest in your own life? An inconvenience? A reward? A duty? A successful achievement?

May God grace us to hear him saying to us, "I know what you actually need and I will *give* it to you.

May we be filled with anticipation for this great gift, and unpack the gift with enthusiasm and great hope. And may we learn to use the gift, engage it regularly, and be filled with delight.

Day 4
When do we need rest?

It might seem like an odd question to ask, but "When do we need rest?" Isn't it obvious? Many of us would say that we *need* it right now, but we just can't get any right now. There is simply too much on our plates to rest *now*.

But this is precisely when rest comes into its own. Now. We need it precisely when we're struggling to keep up with multiple calendars and kids' sports and family meals and *all the things.* We need rest right now when life is so full and so busy.

That might sound impossible or unrealistic, but isn't a gift *most appreciated* when it's *most needed?*

Yes, *if* we recognize the need.

I'm often given books as gifts. I receive at least two books a month, and sometimes far more. And while I truly love books and am often genuinely excited to receive them, I've noticed an interesting distinction in the way I handle these gifts. Most, after a quick glance at the cover and a brief skim of the table of contents, get shelved. And that's where they remain; categorized, stored, but unused. Sometimes, however, I am so compelled by a book that I start it immediately. I carry it with me hoping to read a few pages in spare moments between appointments. I might complete it within days, and talk to others about the content, and put what I learned into practice.

What's the difference between the shelved books that I don't read, and the well-marked, shared-with-others, and *lived* books?

My recognition of my need.

If I'm currently grappling with a question that the book addresses *and I recognize that,* I read it *right now.* In other words, when I'm given a gift that addresses an actual need, I use the gift immediately.

When do I most need food? When I'm working really hard. Ironically, when I'm working really hard, I sometimes forget to eat, but my forgetfulness doesn't diminish my need.

When do I most need rest? Precisely when I'm going, going, going and have been running at full speed for too long; too long in a day or too long in a week or too many weeks on end.

Ironically, when I'm scheduled morning to night and keep adding even more responsibilities, I sometimes forget to rest. And when I forget long enough, *I don't even recognize the need* anymore. But the need persists.

What would it look like for you to build some intentional rest into today, this week, or this month? Have you forgotten you need it *now*? Your forgetfulness does not diminish your real need.

We can't wait until the demands, pressures, and busyness of life ease so that we can rest. Rest is not something we might one day get to. It is the gift of God that enables us to flourish in each day.

A gift is most appreciated when it's most needed. It is also most powerful and formative at such times. Perhaps today you might say or pray: "This is exactly what I need right now. Not after this busy season, but right in the middle of it. *Thank you.*"

Day 5
Bone-tired and stressed out

Weary.

Jesus said to the crowd following him, "Come to me all you who are weary" (Matthew 11:28). The original Greek word that we translate as *weary* means to be tired from toil, burdens, or grief. It primarily refers to our physical condition, for which we might more commonly use the word *exhausted*.

This is the same word used by Peter in Luke 5:5 when he said, "Master, we've *worked hard* all night and we haven't caught anything…" He literally says, we've *wearied* ourselves all night. Many of us can relate to that feeling. It's also the word used in John 4:6 when John notes, "Jacob's well was there, and Jesus, *tired* as he was from the journey, sat down by the well."

Weariness speaks to our physical condition. Our bodies are weary. We feel bone-tired, and it runs deep within us.

That's whom Jesus is addressing when he says "Come to me all you who are weary….", but it's not just the physically exhausted to whom he speaks. Jesus adds, "*…and burdened.*"

Burdened.

The word translated *burdened* seems to speak specifically to the pressure associated with unattainable expectations or impossible rules. It perhaps refers to the emotional weight that many of us feel so acutely.

Burdened might describe the kind of pressure felt by some Jews in Jesus' day to keep the hundreds of extra religious laws. Or it might describe the kinds of pressures potentially felt by some of us today to be "perfect parents" when we constantly make mistakes, or the pressure to be "successful at what we do" when we're hardly keeping things together, or the pressure to be consistently "good" when we're actually struggling with sin.

A word that we use more commonly than burdened is *stressed*. While we might feel weariness in our bodies, we feel burdened in our souls. It's one thing to have a weary or tired body. It's a different thing to have a burdened spirit, or a heavy heart, or "a lot on my mind."

Weary speaks to a physical load. *Burdened* speaks to an emotional load. Jesus gently invites us: *"Come to me, all who are weary and burdened."* He speaks to all of us who feel bone-tired and stressed-out.

I recently spoke with a dentist who told me his business has never been better. Curious, I ventured a few theories, "Are people not brushing?" "Refusing to floss?" "Drinking too much soda?" He leaned closer like he was about to reveal a secret. "People are so stressed they are breaking their own teeth!"

Are you weary and burdened? Are you feeling exhausted and stressed? Is the pressure of your emotional burden destroying you physically? If your answer is "Yes," Jesus has a word for you. "Come to me."

That's the solution. Before we talk about sleep and exercise and boundaries and work/life balance Jesus says, "Come *to me*." Why? Precisely because we don't come to him when we're weary and burdened.

Where have you been going for rest and solace? For a few minutes of distraction or recuperation? Today, try coming to Jesus a few times. He promises to restore us.

Day 6
A design plan or design flaw?

It's vital to realize that God created us with needs. He designed us for dependence.

Our need for oxygen, which will become urgently apparent if we hold our breath for a minute, is not a design flaw. It is a design plan. We were built to breathe.

Our need for food, which our body will remind us about multiple times each day, is not a design flaw. It's the way we were made. God engineered us to eat.

Similarly, you were made to need rest. Rest is part of the design which God called "good."

Being well-rested is critical for mental alertness, physical performance, and relational connection, not to mention spiritual acuity. But we are so seldom well-rested that many of us have normalized tiredness. Exhaustion has become our common companion. Nevertheless, our elevated heart rates, muscle cramps, skin breakouts, brain fog, sickness, moodiness, difficulty sleeping, and inability to be still and silent, are all warning lights on our personal dashboards alerting us to the fact that *we need rest.* The warning lights warn that we are not living as we were designed.

I'm startled to realize how deeply I've been shaped by a subtle cultural falsehood; that my need for rest is a sign of weakness. I confess that I view rising early as a mark of maturity, productivity as a measure of value, and grit as a characteristic to be celebrated. None of these things are bad, in and of themselves, but they are deeply embedded cultural values which I've prized to the point of denying (or at least neglecting) my God-given need for rest.

Over time I've related to rest more as an enemy than as a gift; more of an inconvenience than part of my fundamental God-ordained design.

None of my mentors have been good at resting. One used to respond to suggestions that he take an occasional break from working so hard by saying, "There's plenty of time to rest on the other side!"

I love to view life as a battle and myself as a valiant warrior in it. Big challenges and calls to sacrifice motivate me, and I find it easy to believe the solution to most problems is simply working harder. But truthfully, I'm tired. I'm weary. I'm burdened. I wonder whether my pace is sustainable. To be honest, I need rest. Gratefully, that's a good thing.

Our need for rest is hardwired into our humanity. We are not the less for it. Indeed, to ignore it or deny it, is to become less than God intended.

What mindset might you need to challenge within yourself today? And how might you restore the design rather than violate it today?

Day 7
False assumptions about rest

"Come to me," Jesus says, "and I will give you rest."

We often assume that Jesus means "*Stop*"; stop moving, stop working, stop laboring, stop stressing, stop performing, stop doing anything. We can easily mishear him, but Jesus is not instructing us to stop permanently, as though there is nothing to do. Rather, the invitation is to pause and redirect our attention *for a short time* in order to recover, in order to regain strength, in order to be refreshed.

Jesus is saying, I want to give you what I created you to need in order to do the work I created you to do. You have work to do; I have rest to give.

As we noted earlier, one false assumption about rest is that it's something we deserve and get to enjoy once the work is done. It's our reward. The assumption is that rest is primarily related to what has *already happened*, not to what needs to happen still.

Many of us are familiar with American

football. In that game there are unlimited substitutions. At the end of every play, teams can put new players in and take other players out.

One of the reasons a coach might take a player out is because the player needs rest. But the assumption is that the player, once they get a breather, some water, and some rest, will go back on the field and continue to play, because the game isn't over. There's more work to be done. They get rested not because of what they have just done, but because of what remains to be done.

One of the more obvious reasons some of us find rest so difficult is that there's so much work to be done. Yet, Jesus is not arguing that point. Of course, there's more work to be done. And of course, he knows that. But what he's saying is "Before you do more work, rest. Before you return, recover. Sit this play out, so you can give it your all for the next three plays."

Jesus invites the physically weary to receive rest for physical recovery. And while physical rest is good and needed, Jesus is clearly also talking about rest from emotional burdens, grief and sadness, pressures to perform, and the heaviness that comes with responsibilities that may not quickly, if ever, go away.

For many of us, these burdens will be there again tomorrow. In other words, you may live with this grief for a while. You may work under this pressure for years. Life seems to come with a certain set of burdens. The gift is that even *in the midst* of long journeys with physical, emotional, or spiritual burdens, Jesus is offering rest. It is not rest at the end of the journey, but rest *in order to continue* the journey.

There's a lot more work to be done. That's why we need to rest.

It's a false assumption that rest means weakness, or that rest means prolonged or permanent retreat from life. Similarly, it's a false assumption that rest is just about recovery from the past days, weeks, or months.

Today, how might you apply this idea of rest as a sign of strength, and as your best preparation for this afternoon, tomorrow, or next week?

Day 8
Perceived hindrances to rest

We may have a variety of hindrances to real rest, a whole stack of reasons why we have so much trouble receiving or even valuing this gift. Which of the following statements might describe your perception of rest?

Rest isn't important.

At our core, some of us aren't actually convinced of rest's value, or whether rest is a valid or valuable use of time. Nearly every other activity feels more urgent or more important than resting. Perhaps over time, we have come to believe that rest is what happens when nothing else needs to be done, but there's always something else that needs to be done.

Or perhaps you tend to think that…

Rest is laziness.

Some of us grew up in households that modeled busyness, extolled hard work, rewarded diligent effort, and valued achievement. We came to believe, deep in our hearts, that rest is an excuse for laziness. Consequently, when we hear people speak of needing rest or taking rest, we might question their performance or capacity. "Perhaps they're lazy," we wonder. And for some of us, laziness is akin to a mortal sin. We hate laziness and think less of people who *are* lazy. It makes rest hard for us.

Or perhaps you have come to believe that…

Rest is irresponsible.

Even if we believe rest is valid, some of us feel that we simply don't have the freedom to rest (or the freedom to stop working) because to stop working, especially if we are parents of young children or business-owners or full-time caretakers, means the needs of others might go unmet. If we miss a dance rehearsal for our pre-teen, it might create an irrecoverable hurt. If we ask a client to wait, we might lose the sale. If we don't get mom's meal ready precisely when she wants it, people might think we are uncaring, heartless, or irresponsible.

Perhaps you'd like to rest, but resting feels wrong because delaying the meeting of others' needs feels irresponsible.

Or maybe you're convinced that…

There's simply not enough time for rest.

Some of us, even if we appreciate the value of rest and believe it's possible to rest responsibly, don't know where rest could possibly fit into our schedule. Any form of planned rest just feels like an unattainable luxury. The schedule is completely full, every single day. There is literally no room for anything else. Our calendars are already totally filled up. We simply do not have the time.

What shall we do? Will these misperceptions continue to rule and ruin our lives?

Perhaps a first step is to identify and name the attitudes that we carry about rest. These damaging perceptions run deeply within us, probably formed by our family of origin, our childhood experiences, or influential peer groups growing up. And until we can name the chain that binds us, we will struggle to live into the true freedom of rest.

Are these hindrances part of your story?

Day 9
I'm not ready to rest

Unready.

Practically, this is the biggest shift I need to make in order to recover meaningful and effective times of rest: I need to prepare to rest.

That may sound silly, especially if you see rest as *doing nothing*, but it's a lot easier to let *nothing* get squeezed out of the calendar than something.

If someone asks "What are you doing tomorrow morning?" and my answer is "Nothing," then it's so easy to get pulled into something that isn't restful. But if the answer to the question, "What are you doing tomorrow morning?" is "I'm resting. I'm going on a walk to rest. I'm heading to the river to rest. I'm visiting my mom to rest. I'm going to rest and read a book… or even if you just keep it vague—"I have plans"—it's *something*.

Resting is not just doing *nothing*. It's purposefully doing something. Consequently, we need to prepare to rest. We need to be ready to rest.

I am best at resting when I plan for it. It's never an elaborate plan. Quite the contrary, it's usually super simple:

- spend the day at the river; or
- leave my phone in the office and eat lunch in the park; or
- pause for five minutes, three times during the day, for prayer.

The "unready" barrier to rest is relatively easy to overcome. It primarily requires planning.

It also means we need to be intentional about working. In order to be ready to rest, we'll likely need to work more effectively and efficiently than we would need to otherwise.

If we've slipped into a pattern of never taking a day to rest, then the shift to taking a day to rest might require working *more*, or more *efficiently*, on six days so we can rest on the seventh.

If we've slipped into a pattern of missing dinner with our family because we're not done with our work, getting home in time for dinner might mean working through lunch or vigilantly refusing distraction while we're at the office, so we are ready to rest when we get home.

If you've had even a little exposure to traditional Jewish culture, you're probably aware of the hurried effort that is often required to finish all the work and prepare all the food before the sun sets on Friday, marking the start of the traditional sabbath. This extra effort is exerted in order to be ready to rest, and to be able to fully rest on Saturday.

It may be sobering to come to terms with the fact that the most common barrier to rest for many of us is that we simply are not ready. We haven't prepared for it. We haven't treated it as *something* on our calendar.

Ironically, *laziness,* our reluctance to work hard with the purpose of being ready for rest, might often be the greatest barrier to rest.

We may need to learn to *work well* in order to be able to *rest well*. It's reasonable to expect some level of preparation to be required in order to be ready to practice the discipline of rest and receive the gift of rest.

Might it help if you marked rest on your calendar as an appointment to keep?

Getting ready for rest is not about running ourselves into the ground until we collapse. It's about creating regular time and space for the health of the body, heart, mind, and soul.

Day 10
I'm not able to rest

Some seasons of our lives are so frenetic, so all-consuming, so utterly demanding that we can't rest. There's so little time or opportunity, it seems.

Raising children can feel like that; constant go, go, go. Running your own business can feel like that; so much to do to get it off the ground and keep it running. Single-parenting (one of the hardest jobs in the world) can feel like that. Caring for someone with deep needs can feel like that. Working two jobs to make ends meet can feel like that. When is a person supposed to rest? We *can't* rest.

In our hearts we know that rest matters as much now as ever. But restorative time can be hard to find—sometimes *impossible* to find. Here are two thoughts to consider.

First, rest is not simply "time off." The restoration of the soul is not just a product of downtime, but of differently used time. "*Come to me…*" said Jesus "*…and you shall find rest for your souls.*" Yes, it's possible to find rest not just after the storm but in the middle of the storm.

It's possible for our souls to be replenished not just after the work is done, but while the work is being done, with short asides of coming to Jesus. Have you tried that? It's a discipline that can become a restorative habit and produce a constantly renewing life.

As we know well, rest for the soul is not the automatic byproduct of sitting on a couch for hours with a drink in one hand and the television remote in the other.

Downtime is not always restorative time, but there *are* times when we need to lay down the burden, take a break from the demands, and recover a fresh perspective. What happens when we simply cannot find those hours in a week, or days in a month?

Today, take a few minutes at regular intervals throughout the day to turn again to Jesus. You might be surprised how he meets you and restores you in the midst of your busyness.

Here's a second thought for consideration. God gave the sabbath command (Exodus 20; Deuteronomy 5) to a nation, not a person. Yes, people individually practiced it, but it was most possible because they were collectively committed to it. Sometimes we need each other to make rest possible.

When I cannot rest because of the weight of expectations, I might need you to lift some of the weight for me.

This reinforces why Christian faith *and rest* is best experienced and practiced within a community. We are not designed to go it alone. It was not God's intention or plan that we should grind out each day by ourselves.

This begs two questions: Are we willing to let others serve and support us if we simply cannot create restful space on our own? And conversely, are we willing to step into the lives of others—our kids, friends, church, or local community—to create space for them to experience rest and restoration? Thriving lives depend on it.

This might involve (for example) babysitting, meal-making, or caregiving; supportive acts that can easily be done within families and between friends. No program necessary. It's driven by a simple, fundamental, and profound motivation; the restoration of human lives. And perhaps with this rest people will find fresh space and new capacity to hear God and experience his grace.

When we are not able to rest, perhaps we could start by snatching moments with Jesus. Or perhaps it's time to call in the cavalry of the community. Is there a next step for you here?

Day 11
I'm not willing to rest

Discovering the real reasons why we're weary and burdened will likely call for blunt and merciless introspection. No excuses! Actually coming to terms with what's really at the core of our weariness and stress will require us to be uncommonly honest with ourselves. And then actively addressing these core reasons for our exhaustion will likely demand some difficult work. Why is that?

Most of us will find that the real barrier to receiving the gift of rest is not a lack of knowledge, but a lack of desire. Most of us, much of the time, are simply *unwilling* to come to Jesus to receive what our souls truly need.

It's not that we don't have time to pray. The truth is we don't feel like praying.

It's not that receiving the gift of rest is impossible. The truth is we choose not to prioritize time with our Creator. We simply don't want to.

For many of us the real barrier to rest is that we think we know better than God. Of course, we'd hesitate to admit this. Intellectually we're usually willing to admit that God knows best. But *emotionally* (and most of us live more from our emotions than from our intellect, especially when it comes to what we *want*) we prioritize our *preferences*. We want it our way. We want to live the way we want to live, eat what we want to eat, do what we want to do, and relax the way we want to relax, especially when we're tired. We typically opt for mind-numbing entertainment and unhealthy comfort food. And we do this *repeatedly*.

It's sobering to admit it. But the truth may be that we actually *don't want* to respond to Jesus' invitation, "Come to me…"

Lord have mercy.

Here's the good news. Jesus knows us completely, loves us unconditionally, and invites us unreservedly into an honest relationship.

We can repent of the pride that pushes our time with Jesus way down the list of priorities.

We can pray, "I do believe; help my unbelief." We can even pray, "I *want* to want you more." Similarly, we can confess that we often don't want to come to Jesus when we're weary and burdened. We can ask for a stronger desire for intimacy with Christ.

The good news is that God is a good Father who loves us and wants to give us good gifts. Jesus says, "If you then, though you are evil, know how to give good gifts to your children, how much more will your Father in heaven give the Holy Spirit to those who ask him!" (Luke 11:13) In other words, we can admit our need and ask God for help, even to desire God.

So, when we're exhausted and stressed out and we know that we need something more substantial than a movie and some ice cream, but we truthfully lack the desire to come to Jesus we should honestly admit it and pray, simply,

> "Jesus, help me come to you to receive the gift of rest for which my soul is truly longing. Empower me to look to you for help even as my willpower is weak."

Day 12
Human machines versus human beings

Perhaps you remember those TV ads that featured the Energizer bunny. The toy drummer bunnies were loaded up with batteries from various manufacturers and then set in motion. In the marketing videos, the Energizer bunny was still beating and moving long after the other bunnies stopped.

In our family, we described someone who moved constantly as an "Energizer bunny." It was a compliment. They apparently didn't need rest. They could press on when others ran out of fuel. And over time this compliment for others quietly and subtly became an expectation for myself. We never vocalized it with these precise words, but we believed that the most impressive people were like machines. They just kept going.

Such thinking has been detrimental in so many ways. It undermined my own sense of self-worth. If I couldn't perform constantly, endlessly, then I felt inferior in some way. It undermined my assessment of other people. If they couldn't keep going, and keep going at a pace that I respected or admired, then I neither respected nor admired them. It compelled me to work harder than anyone else; first to the office and last to leave. It drove me into exhaustion which impacted my family and friendships. It became a distorted badge of pride that made illness (forced rest) or vacation (extended rest) sources of irritation or (ironically) restlessness.

Energizer bunnies don't stop, lest they be mistaken for inferior bunnies.

All of this reflects a very broken understanding of humanity. We are not machines, designed to work at a high pace day after day, season after season, year after year. We are human beings.

Machines are purely utilitarian. They serve some useful purpose for us and we only keep them as long as they're getting the job done. As soon as the machine breaks down, slows down, or wears out, we pop it in the garage or discard it.

Human beings, on the other hand, are not useful tools. They are, as the phrase indicates, *beings.* They have profound value just because they exist; because they *are*.

When machines break down, we might call a service technician who can identify a broken part or a worn fitting and quickly replace the faulty piece.

When human beings break down, the process of restoration is far more complex and there is often irreparable damage.

Machines can become obsolete, even if they are working. Subsequent technology can render earlier technology irrelevant and useless. Anybody still got a working cassette player from the 1980s?

Human beings do not have planned obsolescence built into them by God. We are made in his image, and have a fixed value; unalterable and eternal.

Everything about the machinery model is destructive to our humanity, and yet we apply it so quickly, deeply, and frequently to ourselves and the people around us. Do we have the confidence to shake it loose and to sincerely embrace our humanity?

We won't quickly make this shift in thinking. But if we could reject the *machinery mentality*, we might find ourselves more open to rest and more gracious with others.

How might you better embrace your *being* as much as your *doing* today?

Day 13
Ending slavery

Work is good.

God created Adam and Eve to care for the garden. The curse, after their sin, was not that they'd now have to work, but they would work "by the sweat of their brows" (Genesis 3:19). They'd be fighting against the earth. The earth itself would no longer cooperate, and good work would become hard toil.

We've all experienced the subtle shift from life-giving productivity to life-sucking effort. Initially, it might happen just from time to time; a hard day here, a bad day there. Then gradually, almost imperceptibly, it increases and one day we feel utterly depleted and realize that the tank is empty, but we can't stop this train. Perhaps we need the money. Or the accolades overshadow the emptiness. Or the promotion just can't be handed back. We're stuck.

When Moses received the Ten Commandments from God, he recorded two different reasons for the fourth commandment ("Observe the sabbath"). In Exodus 20, it's because God himself rested on the seventh day during the creation week. But in Deuteronomy 5, we read a different reason: "[Observe the sabbath so that] you shall remember that you were a slave in the land of Egypt, and the Lord your God brought you out of there by a mighty hand and an outstretched arm."

It's entirely possible to enslave ourselves to our work, and such slavery will always diminish us. Our work will often take as much as we'll offer and we may look there for our significance and legacy.

But think of the typical workplace. Two weeks after we're done—for whatever reason—even after many years of hard toil and faithful service, our names will hardly be uttered again. Organizations and businesses don't make profit by sitting around and endlessly honoring past workers. They replace them quickly and press on with the business of the day. Meanwhile, we may have sacrificed our marriages and families. We may have neglected our spouse and children. We bought the hollow promise of significance which dangled endlessly in front of us like the proverbial carrot. Yet, when the dust settles, we realize that our work produced a far smaller legacy than we imagined or hoped for.

We were slaves. Slaves, indeed. Yes, we were paid, and perhaps paid well. But slavery describes a condition of the soul not the bank account. Slavery is marked not by the office size or title at work but by the damage done to the soul.

The sabbath, a day of rest each week, is more than a day off. It's a day to remember and to reorient. It's more than a day to sleep in. It's a day to recall who you are and to resist the subtle servitude that can steal our deepest joy. It's a day for at least brief reflection that we are not defined by our efforts or made valuable by our skills.

A flourishing life embraces work but is ever wary of slavery.

Today, consider how much your work defines you. Does it serve you or do you serve it? Would a sabbath rest help you remember that Christ has set you free from slavery?

Day 14
Be still in the storm

Unlike explanations of doctrine or records of historic events, the Psalms are songs written for worshiping communities to sing and experience together. Songs aren't really meant to be studied—they're meant to be sung. Poems are like that as well. They intend to express emotion and explore truth in evocative language.

Psalm 46, as an example, is a short worship song with three parts, and at the end of each part appears an untranslated word, *selah*. This word is not completely understood but most scholars think it is an indication that those singing the song should pause and reflect for a moment on the words that they're singing.

If you spend much time in the Psalms, you will find their honesty quite riveting. Emotionally, they're raw and unfiltered. They break the rules, so-to-speak, of what you might expect in a worship service. There is, apparently, no effort to soften language or avoid doubt or despair or to hold back when the writers feel life is unfair or that God isn't stepping in.

And some of these raw, honest prayer songs include a few *selahs*, a few *pauses*. The purpose of these pauses is not to take a break *from* the emotion being expressed in the song but to rest *in* the emotion. It's to feel it. It's to soak in it. It's to rest in it.

The invitation is to bring all of this real life stuff to God and then to rest. It's to express the burdens of your heart, and then be still. It's to let it all out, and then let it all go.

Many of the psalms are songs to God but they're more than that. They are conversations with God where we cry out, we yell and shout, and then we rest and listen. We say what is on our mind, and then we pause and ask God to speak.

The assuring truth declared in the final movement of Psalm 46 is that God is God. All of life is in his hands. Consequently, the invitation to those singing is to "be still and know that I am God."

You've likely heard that invitation before. I wonder what the context has been. You may have seen it painted as art in a friend's kitchen. You may have read it printed on a sympathy card. And perhaps, at times, you've read those words with a dose of cynicism and thought, "That's a convenient idea to ponder while you sip a latte with peaceful piano music playing softly in the background."

Perhaps the reason for your cynicism is that you're in a battle. You might be in the fight of your life. It might feel like things are falling apart. And what gets lost when we pull that key verse ("Be still and know that I am God") from the rest of the psalm is exactly what makes it so radical and so powerful.

God doesn't say, "Be still and know that I am God" while you're walking on the beach or picking flowers in a field. Well, he might, but that's *not* what's happening in Psalm 46.

What's happening in Psalm 46 is complete upheaval. These powerful words are made even more powerful when we recognize they are an invitation given in the midst of chaos, in the middle of the night, when God's people are completely exhausted.

God says "Be still" when everything is falling apart, when we're not sure things can get worse, when we're wondering with increasing certainty if our current struggle might, in fact, be the fatal blow.

Psalm 46 begins with a powerful declaration of belief, "*God is our refuge and strength, an ever present help in times of trouble*" followed by an emotional choice: "*Therefore we will not fear.*"

But the following verses list a litany of *fearful things*, including earthquakes, floods, and militarized national upheaval. The writer considers how to respond to life-altering events, terrifying realities, and frightening twists to our lives.

The Psalmist is well-acquainted with the battle, the fight, the struggle, the hard work, and the anguish of the night.

But in this song, when the dust settles, a new dawn breaks forth. And in the morning light we see God standing, unmoved, good, and victorious. And we, with the Psalmist, realize that we don't have to keep fighting. We can rest. We can *be still*.

The word ("*be still*") in the original language carries the idea of loosening our grip or unclenching our fist. The fight is over. The warrior can drop his sword. One translation puts it like this: "*Let go* and *know* that YHWH is God."

When can we let go? After the battle? No. *In the midst of it.* You can let go right now. God has been faithful in the past. God will help you in the future. And God is God right now.

We can be still even while battles rage. Even in the chaos, we can rest. We can let go and know that God is God. Selah.

Day 15
Rest for the soul

As we've already noted, the opening pages of the Bible declare that rest is built into the very fabric of the created order. It is part of God's design, and it is a gift.

On the seventh day of creation, God himself rested (Genesis 2:2). He ceased from his work, not because he was weary but because there is something fundamentally good, powerfully restorative, refreshingly centering, and importantly true about rest.

Rest is not wasted time, nor is it the enemy of productivity. It is not a sign of laziness, nor a luxury for the few. It is core to a flourishing human life. It is essential to our well-being. And while we might agree with those simple declarations, our hearts might also quietly scoff. "Who has time to rest? We can rest when we're dead!"

Might we need to pause and reassess our rest, or lack thereof? Our bodies need it—our minds, too. But there's more to it. Let's return to that powerful and enigmatic statement by Jesus.

"Come to me, all who are weary and heavy-laden, *and I will give you rest*. Take my yoke upon you, and learn from me, for I am gentle and humble in heart; and *you shall find rest for your souls*" (Matthew 11:28-29).

Rest for our *souls*?

Perhaps that's the rest we need most today. Our bodies and minds need rest, for sure. But our souls need it at an even deeper level. And Jesus points the way.

This rest is not attained by gaining special knowledge, doing advanced spiritual exercises, or adding an hour or two of weekend leisure to our lives.

Interestingly, Jesus does not talk with his disciples about time-management, self-care, or setting better boundaries. He says, ever so simply, "*Come to me.*" Have we really heard this simplest and most promising of all invitations?

He says, "*Come to me…*" and we proceed to *go to* all sorts of other places looking for rest and relief. We *go to* sports, Netflix, shopping,

Cinemark, food (lots of it), medication, exercise, yoga, and counseling.

"*Come to me…*" That can't be enough. There must be more. What's the real secret of rest? Where can I find genuine restoration and lasting relief? Jesus makes it simple. "*Come to me.*" It's something we can all do. It doesn't take money, education, great ability, grit, or determination. We just show up *for him*. We come *to him*. We hang out *with him*.

Feeling exhausted?

God doesn't demand that we rest. Instead, he gently, persistently, graciously invites us into his rest; every day. "*Come to me…and you will find rest for your souls.*"

This rest not only rejuvenates us in the deepest places. It also forms us. This rest is not only about sustaining our bodies and minds for today, but forming us for eternity.

Body-weary is one thing. Soul-weary is next level. When our souls feel utterly depleted, where shall we go? There is no therapy that restores the soul. Just faith and the balm of God's presence.

How might you come to Christ today, more consciously and more constantly? How might you practice his presence throughout the day? How's your soul?

Day 16
The rest stop is not our destination

My wife and I enjoy road trips. Spending time together, hours of it, driving to familiar or new places is a joy.

One summer we planned a road trip from Northern California out to Yellowstone National Park (Wyoming). We knew where we would stop each night and we designed a large loop that brought us back through Boise, Idaho (where friends live) and then through a part of Oregon and California we had never seen. It was a glorious trip that included a little fly fishing, a lot of buffalo, and amazing new sights.

Now I ought to make a confession. I've often been a "drive till you drop" kind of guy. I don't like stopping for gas and have been known to limp into a station with little left in the tank but fumes. And who needs to stop for large meals en route? Food merely delays progress. But in recent years, I have discovered a lovely feature along the U.S. interstates. They're called "rest stops."

Not all rest stops are created equal, however. Indeed, we've driven past plenty that were under construction, and others that definitely could use some attention. But there is usually a cluster of trees, a relatively clean bathroom, and a board with a map or other local information.

Some rest stops have just the basics. Others turn out to be a great surprise. Traveling to Idaho from Wyoming we came upon a rest stop in the Craters of the Moon National Monument and Preserve (in Idaho) that turned out to be a wonderful and fascinating tourist stop. We turned off the main road and dropped down behind an embankment and found dozens of cars and a full indoor welcome center, replete with captivating videos about the history of the region and the stunning fields of lava rock that stretched for miles. It was a find, largely invisible from the road.

I'm grateful for the rest stops—truly. And the older I get, the more grateful I am. It's helpful to stretch the legs and take a break from driving.

But the rest stop is just that—a rest stop. It is not the destination. The rest rejuvenates me and allows me to keep driving with fresh energy and focus. Even on those couple of occasions when I have been on my own and slept at a rest stop overnight, I still didn't plan to stay there permanently. It was temporary.

That's how rest works, doesn't it? We are designed for work and productivity. There's something soul enriching about creativity and travel and building and effort. Those things that tire us are often also things that also motivate us and bless us. (Think about raising children.) But when the rest stops show up along the way, they are welcome and we would do well to pause.

What do the rest stops in your life look like right now? Do they come with sufficient frequency? Do they need some maintenance? Do they have spaces to inform and refresh you?

How's your road trip going? Perhaps today you'll be able to pull off the road for a few minutes instead of just pushing on relentlessly. There could be a surprise or two just behind that embankment. And Christ may meet you there.

Day 17
Rest from the noise

I glanced down as my Apple watch buzzed on my wrist. It was announcing that the decibel levels in that worship service had spiked to an unsafe level. There was not much I could do about it; just ride it out. It was only going to be a few minutes.

The alert was helpful. It made me mindful of potentially deafening noise. And while that is important, a few moments of *deafening* noise might be less of a threat to me than the constant *deadening* noise in my life.

We live in arguably one of the noisiest eras of human history. It's constant. Earbuds and headphones abound while we exercise, walk, or work. We turn on TV sets early in the morning and again late at night. Our phones beep, buzz, and vibrate with regular notifications, while we frequently watch video clips (Facebook, Instagram, or YouTube), play video games, or listen to news reports. We play music or podcasts while we drive, and many places that we visit will have digital screens endlessly playing sports or shows.

Nobody sits still for long, and if we do we immediately fill the space with noise. But the environmental noise is just part of the danger. The internal noise, within our heads and hearts, is equally real and draining.

Have you found yourself unable to switch off the replay button? You know, that persistent replay reel of a hurtful conversation you had recently? Or perhaps it's the rehearsal button that seems stuck going over what you'll say when you next meet that person? Love can do that. So can pain or fear.

Perhaps one reason we embrace so much external noise is precisely because we want to escape the uncomfortable *internal* noise that might other-wise overtake us. We are a culture uncomfortable with silence.

The noise distracts us from unwelcome thoughts. It also numbs us momentarily from our loneliness and fears.

By stark contrast, the Christian tradition of spiritual formation has always extolled the value of silence and solitude. Yet, we resist it.

In silence and solitude we are likely to face the least comfortable version of ourselves. Silence and solitude can function like a spiritual spotlight, exposing things within us and about us that we prefer to leave piled in dark corners. In silence and solitude we might also face demons and a whole new level of spiritual conflict. St. Benedict once wrote that when the ancient desert fathers and mothers sought silence and solitude they engaged in hand-to-hand combat with the Adversary. That can certainly happen.

But in silence and solitude we are also more likely to encounter God. The still soul is more likely to hear the soft voice of God, and sense the gracious beckoning of Christ.

Let's have no illusion. Our flesh will always desire noise, but our souls will flourish most after seasons of silence and solitude. There's nothing easy about a stint in the wilderness (ask Jesus) but we too easily underestimate the transformational power of getting away to "a quiet place."

Is the noise deadening you? Perhaps there's an ancient path of silence and solitude to explore today. It won't be easy but it might be worthwhile. What small practices of retreat and silence might you build into your life? Rest from the noise might be transformational.

Day 18
Herman Melville's harpooner

In his retelling of a scene from Herman Melville's famous story *Moby Dick*, Eugene Peterson described the climactic moment of a whale hunt. The ship is on the chase and the whale is breaching in the distance. The sailors are rushing around deck hauling on the sails, ensuring that everything is prepared to retrieve the whale once it is shot. It's a bustling scene, full of chaos and activity.

But one person is largely inactive — the harpooner. He sits by the harpoon watching the whale spouting in the distance and preparing himself to take the shot. Everything about being at sea depends on him successfully taking that shot. If he misses with the harpoon, nothing else matters. He will have failed his purpose and the entire crew will have failed their mission.

It's imperative that the harpooner rises to his task from a place of rest. His heart rate will already be sufficiently high, without joining all the distraction and activity elsewhere. If the harpooner decides to rush around the deck and then stop ever so briefly to collect himself before firing the rope-attached harpoon, he will be far less likely to succeed. Stillness and calmness are key to a careful and successful shot.

To uninitiated sailors looking on, the harpooner looks like he's not pulling his weight or sharing the load. In fact, it's just the opposite. His stillness is required. He must ultimately take the shot from a position of rest, if he hopes to take a *good* shot.

The analogy is almost too obvious in a book like this.

Our lives reflect the chaos of a whaling ship on the hunt. Like those sailors, we are rushing here and there pulling ropes, checking sails, straining at the wheel, or battening down loose items. But when the most strategic moments arise, and they can arise as unexpectedly as the sudden cry of a whale sighting, we need time being still in the harpooner's chair. And that stillness is not an abdication of our duties but a sign of commitment to our greatest duty.

This is true for our marriages, our parenting, our workplaces, and our schools.

Marriages don't thrive when we rush to a

moment of intimacy or deep conversation. They require some stillness.

Parenting that is entirely reactive to the wind and the waves, without time to sit and watch the horizon for a while, is parenting that will ultimately miss some of the most important shots.

Frenetic workplaces that do not allow our hearts and minds to keep pace with our bodies—constantly attached to laptops or phones, for example—become stressful and increasingly unprepared for the moments that matter.

What might the harpooner's seat look like today in your life? Can someone else haul on the sails while you brace yourself for what matters most?

Day 19
Days that start at night

It's a strange rhythm. In the opening chapter of the Bible we read about God creating the world. The text says that God started by separating the light from the darkness. Then "there was evening and there was morning, one day" (Genesis 1:5).

On the second day, God created the expanse, separating waters on the earth from waters above the earth, "and there was evening and there was morning, a second day" (Genesis 1:8).

On day three, God called forth the dry land to appear and instructed the earth to sprout forth vegetation of all kinds. And it was so. "And there was evening and there was morning, a third day" (Genesis 1:13). And so the story unfolds for the rest of that creation week.

What many people miss is that each day starts at night. The day begins in the evening. Why?

Most of us have a very different view of days. We think of starting the day when we wake up. If we ask each other, "Is your day off to a good start?" we mean, "Has everything gone well since you woke up?" Similarly, we talk about the end of the day as that time when we finally turn off the lights and head to bed.

The hours of sleep are not viewed as part of the day. They are lost, in a sense, because we now tend to use the term "day" to describe those hours when we are conscious and in control of what is happening. We make the day happen, and while we need our sleep it is (in our minds) functionally *nothing time*. We certainly want a good sleep but, as many of us might testify, we can't always make that happen. And if sleep proves elusive, we know that the next day might be a bit of a train wreck.

From a biblical perspective, nothing could be further from the truth.

The opening chapter of the Bible clearly indicates that the day starts at night. Did you catch that? *"There was evening and there was morning; another day."* What's going on there?

Might it be God's way of saying that the real start of the day is not when we wake up and take control, but when we lie down and relinquish control to him? "He who neither slumbers nor sleeps" watches over us and does a work within us that we are usually not even conscious of. He nurtures our bodies at the start of the day (the evening) and he speaks to our hearts (sometimes in dreams). He protects us, rejuvenates us, and restores us, and this happens before we do anything for him or for ourselves.

Evening…then morning; a day.

This feels odd to our sensibilities, but it makes total sense. It reinforces the sovereignty of God. This world is first and foremost *his* workplace, not ours. He wants to take the initiative in our lives and with our lives and through our lives.

Our sleep at night is not merely a collapse in exhaustion—though it might often feel that way. It is, to the contrary and in its finer moments, a deliberate surrender to the work of God in us. We can treat sleep like a necessary evil; an interruption to our productivity. Or we might turn it into a more deliberate invitation to God to come and be Lord of our thoughts, dreams, rest, and recovery.

I wonder what might happen if our nightly rest became not just preparation for the next day, but the first part of the day, given over entirely to the Spirit of God? Perhaps we'd find that these are not word games that we are playing, but that we have stumbled onto a key to a flourishing life.

Frederick Buechner once wrote of sleep: "You have given up being in charge of your life. You have put yourself into the hands of the night. It is a rehearsal for the final laying down of arms, of course, when you trust yourself to the same unseen benevolence to see you through the dark and to wake you when the time comes—with new hope, new strength—into the return again of light."

How might you think differently of sleep tonight? As you lay down your head, hand over your heart in a prayer. Let Christ start your day with his work in you.

Day 20
Forced rest

I'm reading a long and theologically intense dialogue, written in the early 5th century between two young monks (John and Germanus) and their superior, the wise and storied Abbot Moses the Black. It's the kind of conversation that would have required an immense amount of energy. The topics are personal and transcendent. The questions explore the dark caverns of human longing, revealing an almost desperate hunger for understanding. The responses are thorough and razor precise. The conversation is not a casual campfire chat, but a full-throttled, unhindered, graduate level discourse for desert monks.

Abbot Moses is giving a master's class to the masters, and they can't get enough. They're drinking from the well of battle-earned soul wisdom and they want another round.

But then Moses says, "Let's rest." John and Germanus resist. How could they possibly sleep after receiving such enlightened insight? They press Moses for more, but he is resolved. They will continue again tomorrow.

After pages and pages of profound spiritual wisdom, it's Moses' simple *rationale for rest* that knocks my too-busy-to-rest personality off its prideful feet.

> *The body will claim everything if denied the little to which it is entitled.*[2]

Jesus, in his goodness, invites us to rest. And as with most invitations, I'm likely to politely decline. I'd love to rest. But I have other things I must tend to. I'd love to rest. But I need to work.

But with increasing volume this warning to care for my body sounds like an alarm. And my habitual refusal to allow my body "the little to which it is entitled" is, I'm afraid, quickly leading me to a place where I must either choose to rest or be forced to rest. I know there will come a point at which my body will simply demand it.

Popular Canadian pastor and podcaster, Carey Nieuwhof, urges people to "take the Sabbath or the Sabbath will take you."

The point here is that in addition to being a gift,

---

[2] John Cassian, Conference One, section 23.

rest is a physical requirement. And if we do not choose to rest, we will be *forced* to rest by our own sick, exhausted bodies and troubled, scattered minds.

In some circles we call that *burnout*. We simply can't go on. The body and the mind just pack it up. They demand *rest*, but with completely depleted reserves, all we can do is *stop*. Forced rest often looks more like totally depleted crashing than measured resting. Wouldn't we be wiser to pause periodically at the aid stations, adding a few moments to our marathon time, than to push past recklessly only to completely collapse before the end of the race?

Are you on the brink of some forced rest in your life? Consider pulling back before the body claims the little to which it is entitled. Please pay attention to this ancient (and deeply Christian) wisdom.

Day 21
A yoke of rest

If Jesus is talking to people who already feel "weary and burdened," why does he use the metaphor of a yoke? In other words, why does Jesus say, "Come to me all you who are weary and burdened…*and take my yoke upon you*"?

The yoke was the heavy wooden collar that joined two oxen together as they plowed a field. It stopped either ox from veering away from the other, or getting ahead of the other. It locked them into step together.

Here's where we usually get confused. We often come to the yoke metaphor from a work perspective, from an achievement perspective, from a performance perspective. We're thinking about all the stuff we're pulling and we hear Jesus say, "Take my yoke" and we think he's got a better system, a superior technology, a smarter way to labor.

But if you read the earliest sermons in Christian history on this passage, you'll quickly realize that Jesus is not talking about a better or more efficient workflow system. Instead, the metaphor speaks to the *humility required* to submit your life to him.

Jesus is talking about the genuine humility it takes to say "Jesus is Lord" *and mean it*. Jesus is talking about a radically changed heart posture that declares, "It's no longer going to be about me. It's all about Jesus. I'm coming under Jesus' yoke. I'm harnessing myself to Jesus. I am all in—100%. I'm surrendering completely. As I died on the day of my baptism, so I'll die every day to my own ambition. I'm relinquishing control. From now on I go where Jesus goes. I walk at Jesus' speed. When Jesus stops, I stop. When Jesus turns right, I turn right. I am *yoked to Jesus*."

It's not that I lose my identity. It's just the opposite. I find my truest and most meaningful identity *in* Jesus.

The yoke is an image of active submission but also active partnership. If I take Jesus' yoke upon myself, then I follow his lead and I live each moment alongside him. What's that mean, specifically? Jesus makes this explicitly clear. "Take my yoke upon you and learn from me, *for I am gentle and humble in heart."*

The word *gentle* describes that disposition of spirit in which we accept God's dealings with us as good, without dispute or resistance.

It's the same word that Jesus uses when he says, "Blessed are the *meek* for they will inherit the earth."[3] It's the same word Matthew uses to describe Jesus riding a donkey into Jerusalem at the start of the Passover, in what is commonly described as the triumphal entry. He quotes the prophet Zechariah: "See, your king comes to you, *gentle* and riding on a donkey."[4]

Being gentle like Jesus means trusting our lives to God, believing that God is good.

Being *humble* like Jesus is renouncing pride. The word humility literally means "not rising far off the ground." Jesus consistently models the gentle humility to which he invites us. Even though Jesus is one with the Father, he willingly submits to the Father.

Here's the point: Being with Jesus — or taking his yoke upon me — will be miserable for me, it will be a constant battle, if I think life is all about me, my way, my desires, my preferences, my identity, my success, and my

---

[3] Matthew 5:5
[4] Matthew 21:5

fame. Because that's not the way Jesus is walking. If I'm going to walk with Jesus and walk like Jesus, I've got to *actually become* gentle and humble. Indeed, the only way to be truly yoked with Jesus is to become *Christlike*.

What attitudes and actions are you tempted to embrace that are clearly not the way of Jesus? Will you, today, resolve to live and work with Jesus, like Jesus, at Jesus' pace?

Day 22
A yoke of companionship

Jesus' invitation to "take my yoke upon you and learn from me" (Matthew 11:29) suggests a powerful insight about *companionship*.

As we noted in the previous chapter, the yoke would connect two oxen so that they might work in the same direction and at the same pace. But the yoke also served an additional purpose. As the two animals worked together, they shared the burden and thereby lessened the load. Their *companionship* within the yoke would motivate them for those more difficult moments when one ox might have quit on its own. The presence of the companion would help the hesitant ox find strength and press on when difficulties arose.

This is the yoke of companionship, and it's so fitting that Jesus would choose this image or metaphor to describe our walk with him. It's not that he needs us but that we, as the weaker partner, absolutely need him. And he guides us straight. He sets a pace we can sustain. And he provides the companionship we need for encouragement, resilience, and persistence.

Is there anyone you'd rather have as a true companion through all of life than Jesus? He is the true lover of your soul, the one who voluntarily died in your place, the victor over sin. Jesus is the conqueror of death. He is the good shepherd, the great physician, the one who walks on water, who calms storms, and who turns water to wine. And he invites us into companionship with him, to play on his team, to work alongside him, to walk step-by-step with him.

It's remarkable.

Jesus invites us into companionship—not a belief system, not a religion, not even just a community, as powerful as that is. What's his invitation? "Come to *me*, and be yoked with *me*. I will give you rest."

When resting is impossible because of so many obstacles, Jesus, gratefully, doesn't prescribe five steps to rest. Instead, he invites us to link arms with him, to be yoked with him. He invites us into companionship.

Of course, there are times when this yoke of companionship might also be shared with the community of Christ-followers. As we bind ourselves to him, he also binds us to each other. Our companionship with other believers is also key to lifting the burdens and exhaustion that we feel.

The yoke of companionship is first with Jesus, but might we also discover that it is a powerful metaphor for the church? Life is never intended to be a solo effort. The burdens are simply too heavy to pull alone. But in this yoke of companionship we discover ourselves moving mountains, first in harness with Christ and then in harness with each other.

Today, how can you take on the yoke with Christ? Or, perhaps you could join the fellowship and companionship of similar yoke-bearers in his name. A burden shared is more than a burden halved.

Day 23
A yoke of grace

Susanna Wesley (1669-1742) was the mother of the founder of the Methodist church John Wesley and his gifted hymn-writing brother Charles Wesley and, if you can believe it, seventeen other children. As you might imagine, raising such a large number of children was a full-time, all-encompassing endeavor.

How on earth might a woman like Mrs. Wesley "come to [Jesus] and receive rest for [her soul]"?

Biographers tell us that Susanna would sit in the kitchen for several minutes each day with her apron flipped up in front of her face and over her head. This is how she'd pray. This is how she found "alone time with God." There was no space away from the chaos. There was no "taking a break" from the demands of her blessed vocation. So, *in the middle of it all*, she'd flip her apron up over her head, come to Jesus, and receive his rest.

What do Jesus' words "*my yoke is easy and my burden is light*" mean for someone like a mother of many children, whose work simply never ends, whose days lack the privilege of predictable patterns, whose abilities are dwarfed by responsibilities?

What is this yoke, this heavy wooden implement that binds the oxen together in work formation, that he invites us to hoist onto our weary shoulders?

In a word, it's *grace*.

That's the brilliant twist here. That's the surprise that Jesus intends for us. He uses a common symbol of weight and burden and urges us to take it up with him because "*my yoke is easy and my burden is light.*" It's a clue.

The common farmyard yoke is heavy and hard, so what could possibly make it light?

Grace.

Here's the irony: We don't bear the weight of grace. Grace bears us. Grace is not a burden that we lift. Grace lifts our burdens. Grace is not an additional responsibility we carry. Grace carries us.

Jesus might have urged us to simply follow in his footsteps, to listen to his teaching, or to mimic his lifestyle as much as possible. But he invites us to put on something, and to join ourselves to him in a surprising fashion. *Put on a yoke of grace.* Receive it and extend it.

Make grace the foundation for the journey and the work ahead. And the effort will indeed be light, not because we will work less or because the burdens aren't heavy but because we will be empowered and guided differently moving forward.

To the weary and burdened, those who have made a habit of carrying the ever-increasing loads of legalism and self-righteousness, Jesus offers not an additional demand, but the free and liberating gift of grace.

We will never truly find rest for our souls until we put on the yoke of grace. Duty chokes us. But grace lifts our heads and our hearts. Sheer responsibility sucks us dry. But grace elevates the spirit within us and inspires hope. Legalism drives us into the wilderness. But grace leads us beside still waters and restores our soul.

Today, how might you put on the yoke of grace and grow in the grace and knowledge of Christ (2 Peter 3:18)? True rest depends on it.

Day 24
Rest and our identity

It's hard to rest when our work defines us. That work need not be paid work. We can pour ourselves into volunteer efforts or raising a family. We can expend our energies pursuing all sorts of ventures, and we'll do so with relentless vigor when our identity is wrapped up in that work.

It's common practice in our culture to ask people whom we meet, "What do you do?" Little wonder, then, that when people ask us that question time after time after time, we gradually feel the pressure to impress. Deep in a corner of our heart, we suspect that we will be assessed in some way for how we spend our lives or how we contribute to society.

Over the years, this has produced humorous new job descriptions, such as some homemakers describing themselves as "domestic engineers." It sounds important and complex which, of course, homemaking *is*.

Retirees often face this challenge quite acutely. When their career is done, it's common for men and women to feel not just a loss of focus and structure that the workplace offered, but a loss of identity. Mothers can face this same dilemma. When the kids are grown and leave home, many moms grapple with identity issues. "Who am I when my life's defining work (to this point) is largely done?"

It's actually both common *and natural* to have to make these adjustments. But this shines a little light on another reason why it can be so hard for us to rest.

The deeper our identity is connected to our performance (wherever that might be, and whatever we might do), the harder it can be for us to lift our foot off the pedal and slow down. If success in our vocation defines our value in society, then rest can pose a threat to that value for some of us.

Nobody finds their identity in rest. Can you imagine being asked what you do and replying, "Oh, I rest a lot!" Who would ever say that? That would be crazy. And the mere fact that it sounds so silly simply reinforces the point. Our significance, at least in our own minds, has nothing to do with rest and everything to do with performance and achievement.

Little wonder, then, that rest is undervalued and under-practiced. It does not contribute in any obvious way to our identity, value, or worth. It's another strike against rest.

But what if we could view rest as intrinsic to our humanity, well-being, and yes, even to our performance and achievement? What if we could view rest not as a threat to our identity but as an indispensable support to it? What if rest was not the necessary evil, but the most necessary good for us to become all that God intended us to be?

You are more than your achievements. You are more than the sum total of whatever you pour your life into. Your value, worth, significance, and identity are not diminished by rest. Quite the opposite. They are magnificently nurtured by rest. It's a paradox. Could this be true? Yes.

How might you reassess your identity today? How might rest, even a little, become a blessing (not a threat) to who you are? This matters. Enormously.

Day 25
Rest and personality

If rest is no threat to our identity, we might equally say that it is not dictated by our personality.

We hear it all the time. "I'm a Type A driven personality, so there's no rest for me." Or, "I'm just hyperactive, so I don't need rest." Or, "I'm a perfectionist, so I am wired to work hard and just keep pushing."

We act as though rest is for certain personality types, but not others. And we might assume that rest matters *least* for the most driven personalities.

Have you taken this view?

Some people certainly seemed wired to be busy. They can hardly stand still. They're always doing something. You might be one of those people, and it can feel like a violation of your nature if you slow down or stop. For you, working "all the time" isn't about identity, it's just your personality.

We can easily acknowledge that we all have different capacities. Our burnout points differ, for sure. Indeed, for some people, sixty hours of work each week is equivalent to forty hours for someone else. The *weary factor*, what we have called *exhaustion* in the title of this book, does not strike us all at the same time, or in the same way, or to the same degree.

But we should have no illusions. While work is built into God's design for us, and work ideally brings us meaning and joy, it is *rest* that rejuvenates the soul…for all of us. The Bible does not differentiate our human needs in terms of personalities.

Gary Smalley, an American family counselor, developed the famous personality trait inventory that aligns us with a lion, an otter, a golden retriever, or a beaver. Have you ever wondered what Adam was? Can you imagine if he and Eve had been two golden retrievers by personality, playing and resting in the garden every day? Perhaps we wouldn't have had such trouble if they had not both been lions!

Of course, that's a playful re-reading of the Bible. But that's precisely the point. Did God not know that human beings whom he created would have such diverse personality traits? Or was personality simply incidental to the sabbath commandment?

Can you imagine, Moses coming down from Mt. Sinai with the Ten Commandments inscribed on stone tablets, and under Commandment #4 ("Remember the sabbath day, to keep it holy") there were multiple subpoints and exceptions and clarifications in fine print for people who were Type A or Type B or ENFP?

We might wonder then if a) the Lord was simply not mindful that some of us would need rest and some of us could skate through without it, or b) whether our personality is not the dominant determinant of our humanity.

Rest is not simply for the slow or low in energy. Neither is it for the relaxed or flexible. It's for all of us, because pausing from our work is not just about recovery, but about worship; not just about rejuvenation but about gratitude. These attributes are independent of personality.

If you are the driven, go-get-'em, take no prisoners, go till you drop kind of personality, you might be surprised by the power of a strategic pause (rest). How might you build that into today?

Day 26
Harmful proverbs

When I was in college, my roommate became renowned for his afternoon naps. They could extend for several hours, and sometimes replaced classes he should have been sitting in. The guys on our residential wing started to put Post-it notes on the door, quoting Scripture. One favorite was, "A little sleep, a little slumber, a little folding of the hands to rest; *and poverty will come on you like a thief, and scarcity like an armed man*" (Proverbs 24:33-34).

We thought it was hilarious, even if it did little to change his habit.

There are plenty of other proverbs in the same vein—proverbs that extol the virtue of hard work and warn against sloth. Indeed, there is warning after warning about laziness: "Laziness makes a person fall into a deep sleep, and an idle person will go hungry" (Proverbs 19:5; CEV).

We may want to recognize that these proverbs have both a light side and a dark side. Laziness may indeed be the downfall of many people. They refuse to work and therefore find themselves without resources for food and shelter. In that sense, laziness is a vice. We don't want to go there.

On the other hand, if we misread the text to mean that we should be working constantly, our workaholism will become a vice of a different kind for which we will pay a significant price.

Might it be true that sometimes we get trapped into assuming that rest and laziness are one and the same? After all, if I say that I am resting, you might conclude "He's not working" and draw a negative inference about me. With such simplistic association (rest equals laziness) we get driven into draining and unsustaining lifestyles. Thus, the Proverbs harm us more than help us.

The problem is not the Proverbs per se, but the way that we hear them through our cultural filter.

We can consider the industrious ants all day long (Proverbs 6:6), but should we not equally consider what Jesus had to say in the Sermon on the Mount?

> See how the flowers of the field grow. They

do not labor or spin. ²⁹Yet I tell you that not even Solomon in all his splendor was dressed like one of these. ³⁰If that is how God clothes the grass of the field, which is here today and tomorrow is thrown into the fire, will he not much more clothe you—you of little faith? ³¹So do not worry, saying, 'What shall we eat?' or 'What shall we drink?' or 'What shall we wear?' ³²For the pagans run after all these things, and your heavenly Father knows that you need them. ³³But seek first his kingdom and his righteousness, and all these things will be given to you as well (Matthew 6:28-33).

It is hard to imagine that Jesus is advocating for laziness or encouraging his followers to quit their jobs or refuse to work. But his words are a perfect counterbalance to the Proverbs which might otherwise drive us to self-reliance, personal kingdom-building, and entire autonomy.

The Proverbs speak to observable truths about life. Hard workers tend to succeed. Sloths suffer. Good people get ahead. The wicked fail. Moral choices hold us in good stead. Immorality will bring us undone. Every religious system and moral code might say the same thing.

But Jesus comes and reminds us that it's a particular kind of diligence and effort that ultimately leads to life and security. "Seek first his kingdom and his righteousness, and all these things [that you worry about so much and work so hard for] will be given to you as well."

Day 27
Helpful metaphors

Sometimes the best way to rethink something is not to think *more* about it but to think *differently* about it. Metaphors can be super helpful in this regard.

When we think of rest, we might consider two metaphors that help us frame it more accurately and more helpfully.

Whitewater Rafting

Have you ever been on a whitewater raft heading down a swollen river with submerged rocks and class III rapids? Imagine for a moment that you are sitting in such a raft, and there in front of you is one of those kiddie steering wheels that we sometimes see on shopping carts. You know the kind. They're plastic. They spin round and round but they are attached to nothing. The child feels like they're steering the shopping cart, but they're really not doing so.

Imagine that on your whitewater raft you have such a fixture. You can quickly see that it is attached to nothing. It makes no difference whatsoever to the direction of the raft. At most it simply gives us a handhold while the raft tosses us to and fro.

Real rest requires us to recognize that much of our life is a river ride, and as much as we want to grab the wheel in front of us (which we perhaps brought with us), it will make no discernible difference. It will not matter whether we strain harder or grip the wheel tighter. We can spin that wheel hard to the right or to the left, but the water will carry us where it wants, regardless of our wheel. Indeed, gripping the wheel is an exercise in futility.

The best course of action is likely to strain less, just hold on, and be prepared to swim if we end up being dumped in the water. We can expend so much energy on things that are nothing but plastic steering wheels in our lives. But rest might actually save our lives if (when) we get tossed overboard.

Does this describe some of the chaos and misguided thinking of your life? It nails me between the eyes. It motivates me to think more deeply about what, when, and where I will expend my limited energy.

Life can be a whitewater rafting trip with a silly plastic steering wheel at each seat.

But there's a second metaphor we might find helpful. It's the image of fallow fields.

Fallow fields

Gino, a friend, does soil conservation for a living. He understands how soil feeds plants and what it takes to rejuvenate soil.

Gardeners like myself, barely know how to differentiate between acidic and alkaline soil. I just keep pumping Miracle Grow on my potted plants and expect…miracles. I assume that potting mix will last forever, and I'm oblivious (sad to say) to the soil's need for rest and recovery. Farmers understand this far better.

Farmers know that fertilizer is enormously helpful for treating the soil and enhancing a crop, but at some point, the soil needs to rest. It needs a break from crop production, so that it can do better, later.

When I see fields sitting with weeds or overgrowth from a season, it looks like nothing much is happening. Indeed, the untreated field can look decidedly untidy and uncared for. But

Gino assures me that this season of rest is not only necessary, it might be the time when the soil is *most active*.

The surface of a resting field might look untended, but what is happening beneath the surface, away from view, is powerfully regenerative and renewing. Indeed, without occasional rest, we can wear out the land. Who knew?

Might these two metaphors provide ways for you to understand your life, your needs, and your efforts in fresh ways, today?

Day 28
Simple practices; difficult habits

Much of this book has invited us to shift our *perspectives* on rest or to "rethink rest", but here are some simple *practices* of rest for you to consider. In time, and with some effort (which may be difficult!), these simple practices can become life-giving habits.

Evening

Choose to let go. Take your hands off the plow. There will be more time to work tomorrow. Now is the time to rest. Now is the time to "be still and know that God is God." Pray.

- Thank God for his goodness.
- Thank God for specific blessings.
- Ask God to establish the work of your heart and hands.
- Lay your worries and concerns at Jesus' feet. Come to him and allow him to care for you.
- *Embrace* the gift of rest.

Morning

Begin with rest. Start the day with a simple, wholehearted acknowledgement of God's presence with you. Center your mind, body, and soul around this profound reality—God is the *giver of life*.

All that you do today will be enabled by God's grace.

- Thank God for his love for you.
- Thank God for the gift of this day.
- Ask God to provide for you and guide you to do good and meaningful work.

Midday

Pause. Set an alarm if you need to. Add the practice of taking just a brief moment around lunchtime to regather the scattered forces of your soul from the pressures and plans, the details, distractions, and disappointments of the morning. And pray.

- Ask God to help you remember that you are his beloved child.
- Ask God for courage and strength to resist temptation and to love well.

Daily

Build a *pattern*. Do what you can to structure your typical day to include some element of renewing rest.

- Build in a coffee break.
- Take a walk at lunch.
- Drive home in silence from work (free from calls, music, podcasts, news).
- Enjoy a family dinner.
- Plan a tech-free evening.

The power of a pattern is the transformational impact over the long-term. Increasingly, even short times dedicated to rest will ground your soul. You'll soon find yourself anticipating them, enjoying them, and becoming more whole through this practice.

Weekly

The entirety of creation is built on a weekly rhythm of rest. You were made to need (and observe) a weekly sabbath.

Choose *one day a week* to pause your normal work. A full day of rest may be impractical in some situations, such as parents caring for young children, but perhaps shorter periods of time can be observed.

Do what you can to live differently on this day. Slow down. Worship. Enjoy good food. Spend quiet time in nature. Read good books. Connect with friends and family. Receive the goodness of God and thank him for the gift of rest and renewal.

Quarterly

Every three months, set apart a day for solitude and personal reflection. Or perhaps include your spouse or a close friend in several hours dedicated to withdrawing, listening, and resting with God.

Consider including structured times of prayer or journaling to help foster an experience that is more than just "time off."

It can be helpful to carry a specific question on which to meditate, or to focus the time on a specific challenge or need.

The goal and hope of these quarterly days away is not to get work done but to create a quarterly rhythm of extended, unhurried, intentional space and time to be with God.

Annually

Perhaps you'd also find great value in reserving a couple of days a year for uninterrupted listening and reflection. These personal retreats invite a deeper level of:

- gratitude for blessings
- surrender of relational responsibilities and life pressures
- clarity of priorities
- creativity
- intentionality, and
- renewing rest.

It will help to move beyond "rethinking rest" to "rediscovering rest" through purposeful action. There is no one-size-fits-all plan. Nor are there formulas whose results are guaranteed. But there is truth *lived*. There are words which we must *put into practice* in order to know their worth.

The Christian spiritual tradition is profoundly rich with rhythms and disciplines and practices and habits which form the latticework of a flourishing life. What might become your "rule of life" for rest?

Day 29
Eternal rest

The writer of Hebrews discusses rest with language that reveals the ultimate issues at stake. Rather than regarding rest as one piece of a healthy life, or one aspect of a balanced schedule, or something to try to prioritize when feeling busy, the writer of this letter sees rest *as a matter of life and death.*

In a dense and sweeping section (Hebrews 3:7 - 4:11), the author touches on three levels of rest: sabbath rest, the Israelites' rest from wandering upon entering the promised land, and eternal rest. By referencing the liberated Israelites' famously tragic failure to realize life in the promised land following forty years of wandering in the wilderness, the author positions rest as the fulfillment of the life of faithful obedience to Christ.

Rest, in other words, was the unrealized hope of the generations freed under Moses, *and* it is the taste of heaven offered to us each week in the sabbath, *and* it is the eternal reality won for all who believe in Jesus Christ.

The writer of Hebrews' argument, simplified,

is this—obedience to God results in eternal rest, while rebellion keeps us from it.

This means that rest is about far more than napping. Rest is about experiencing the fullness of God's good design and grace-enabled plan. That makes rest of profound value.

Furthermore, the failure to experience rest is about far more than *not napping*. The failure to rest is tangled up with rebellion in several forms, including arrogance, anger, and unbelief.

So, I must take seriously the actual dangers associated with not resting. I should see my propensity to ignore God's gift of rest as both foolish and irreverent. Our choice to rest or not rest is an act of the heart as much as it is a choice of the head.

Indeed, rest speaks more profoundly to embracing and realizing our true identity as children of God than we typically realize. As Saint Augustine wrote in his *Confessions*, "Our heart is restless until it rests in you." Therefore, I must continually press deeper into the experience of *resting in God* as critical to both my being and my becoming the person God created me to be.

I must resolutely remove rest from the simplistic, obsolete associations of childhood (it's time for your nap!) or the false assessments of successful adulthood (rest is weakness!). Because, in the biblical view, rest doesn't fit in those limited boxes. Instead, rest is a matter of life and death.

The common and anemic view of heaven as a place of "eternal rest" is nearly completely unattractive because when we think of "rest" we think of sitting. We picture…*nothing*. It's all about what we're *not* doing.

Heaven is far more compelling when we understand "eternal rest" as *fullness of life in God's Kingdom.* We were made for eternal rest, now and forever.

How would you approach rest differently if you understood it as an expression of your identity as a child of God, and as a way of experiencing heaven on earth?

Day 30
Back to Jesus

The solution to this destructive epidemic of exhaustion is not a time management strategy, a change in diet, a reduction of exposure to blue light, more time off, or a new mattress. Each of these ideas may help some of us, at least a little bit, at least for a while. But then we'll need something else.

There is no shortage of proposed "fixes" for the countless symptoms of our exhaustion. The fact that *so many* people feel *so tired* guarantees there will always be another proposed life hack, another pill to purchase, another plan to promote.

But we are so *tired* of all that. Aren't you?

Aren't you tired of the *symptomatic* approach to being tired? Aren't you ready to address the root cause? Aren't you ready to experience rest not simply as a function of well-executed tactics but as a natural, joy-filled byproduct of being whole?

If you are, here's the invitation. It comes directly from the One who designed you and gave you life. It comes from the One who knows you completely, who loves you unconditionally, and who is always only good.

"Come to me" says the Lord and Savior Jesus Christ "and I will give you rest."

Ultimately, the solution is not a plan or a procedure or a purchase. It's a *person*.

The rest we desperately need and truly long for is part of the deep *shalom*—the experience of everything being put right—that can only be known through the person, Jesus.

We, ourselves, cannot earn or attain "rest for [our] *souls*." Only God can give it to us. The good news is he is both willing and able. And he invites all of us to receive this gift.

Throughout this book we have returned repeatedly to Jesus' glorious invitation in Matthew 11:28-30.

> "Come to me, all you who are weary and burdened, and I will give you rest. Take my yoke upon you and learn from me, for I am gentle and humble in heart, and you will find rest for your souls. For my yoke is easy and my burden is light."

These are words to embrace, and words to respond to. Jesus is not just the sage who offers advice. He is the very Source of our rest and well-being. For all of the changes of mindset and new habits that we might choose to implement, it will be for little if not done in partnership with Jesus. We don't come to him for wisdom alone. We come to him, over and over and over again, day in and day out, week by week, and year after year to learn from him (yes!) but also to align with him.

A life out of alignment with Jesus is a life that cannot be in alignment with God's beautiful intent and design. A disciplined life might be an improvement, but only a discipling life will flourish.

Ironically, in this last chapter we return to the first step, because we must not miss it. The first step towards a changed life that can make a difference in your marriage, family, school, or workplace, is to pursue Jesus. If you've not done that, start there now. If you've done that yesterday, then renew that commitment again today, and every day.

And may you experience *shalom*, God's perfect rest.

Made in the USA
Middletown, DE
23 April 2024